Blooming Beautiful

LYNNE LAWER

With thanks to my colouring team who did a wonderful job
bringing to life the photographs on the front cover.

Candise Ham-Warren

Alina Bucur

Donna Sugra

Blooming Beautiful

Colouring in pictures is a great way to relieve stress and it is easy to get amazing results with greyscale photographs. Even a beginner can end up with a picture to be proud of!

If you have never coloured in greyscale photographs before and you would like some help to get the best effects, try using colours that match the shaded areas in depth – use light colours in the lightest areas, dark colours in the darkest places and medium colours in the rest. Having said that, sometimes it looks good if you add a few dark colours in the lightest areas to make them stand out.

Experiment with different colouring media – pencils, crayons, marker pens, paints, even make-up if you feel like it. Put some card or spare paper underneath the page if you are using anything that might bleed through to the next page such as marker pens and paints.

When you do your colouring in, have some relaxing music playing in the background and a cup of tea and a slice of cake to hand if you want to have a completely relaxing time. Enjoy!

© Lynne Lawer

© Lynne Lawer

© Lynne Lawer

© Lynne Lawer

© Lynne Lawer

© Lynne Lawer

© Lynne Lawer

© Lynne Lawer

© Lynne Lawer

© Lynne Lawer

© Lynne Lawer

© Lynne Lawer

© Lynne Lawer

© Lynne Laver

© Lynne Lawer

Ye Olde Crown

© Lynne Laver

© Lynne Lawer

© Lynne Lawer

© Lynne Lawer

© Lynne Lawer

© Lynne Lawer

© Lynne Laver

© Lynne Lawer

© Lynne Lawer

© Lynne Lawer

© Lynne Lawer

About the Author

Lynne Lawer has previously published a greyscale fractal colouring book called Fabulous Fractals that is available to buy from Amazon and the Book Depository. She has split it into five sets of five fractals that can be purchased as digital downloads that you print yourself, from her Etsy store - https://etsy.com/uk/shop/LynneLawerArt

Apart from playing with fractals and photographs, Lynne has enjoyed many other forms of arts and crafts over the years, including jewellery-making, pottery, making fascinators for weddings and dresses for jiving, model-making (out of card), wax art, oil painting, sketching, knitting and crocheting. She is hoping to find the time to try parchment work, card-making, gel candle-making, calligraphy, felting and quilling as she has the equipment already! Ideally, she would like to find a way to combine everything into a fabulous mixed media concoction.

When not working on her books, Lynne loves doing 5D diamond paintings (she adores anything sparkly) or jigsaws on her mobile phone app, preferably while Clyde, the Lawer family's very laidback cat, sleeps beside her.

This is her first greyscale photography colouring book.

If you enjoy Lynne's colouring books, why not join her Facebook colouring group and share your finished pictures? As well as occasional freebies, there will be contests to win digital colouring pages. You may even get the chance to join her colouring team and have your work featured on the cover of her next book! Join the group at -
https://www.facebook.com/groups/1878032522316813

www.ingramcontent.com/pod-product-compliance
Lightning Source LLC
Chambersburg PA
CBHW081630250726
48657CB00009B/2807